Praise for
A Guide to Recruiting
Your Next CEO

As you know, hiring and onboarding a CEO is one of the most important actions a board will ever undertake. So often, even experienced boards struggle to find the right person and are challenged by the process. *I think this book will provide a solid set of guardrails for any nonprofit board in their next search for a CEO.*

David A. Williams, President & CEO
Make-A-Wish America

Dennis' new book is a very useful outline for nonprofit boards of directors of the need for the board to rethink about the whole executive recruitment process, especially since most board members only go through this once or twice. *The risks of getting it wrong are too high.*

Jim Purcell, Chief Executive Officer
Council of Family and Child Caring Agencies of New York

One of the primary responsibilities of a board is to hire a great CEO to lead and push ahead so the organization doesn't become mediocre *This book provides an excellent roadmap to ensure the board recruits a high-performing CEO.*

Jonathan R. Pearson, Executive Director
Corporate Social Responsibility
Horizon Blue Cross Blue Shield of New Jersey

Hiring a CEO is the single most important task a board will ever take on. To find a person not only with the right qualifications, but the right personality, passion for the mission, understanding of the complexities of the nonprofit arena, and leadership skills to inspire both staff and board members, is not an easy task. *This book provides a solid set of fundamentals to guide you in that process and ensure that your next CEO is the right CEO to lead your organization to its greatest potential.* A must-read before you begin the hiring process!

Diana A. Blankman, Senior Director
U.S. Corporate Giving & Social Impact
Novo Nordisk Inc.

Dennis C. Miller has provided a practical roadmap to succession planning, new CEO recruitment and transition of leadership. He offers many insights into excellent management, planning and coordination by board members. *It's a must-read for board members and CEOs in the nonprofit sector.*

Charles Venti, President
Inventive Strategies, LLC

A Guide
to Recruiting
Your Next CEO

Other Books by Dennis C. Miller

A Guide to Achieving New Heights:
The Four Pillars of Successful Nonprofit Leadership

The Nonprofit Board Therapist:
A Guide to Unlocking Your Organization's True Potential

The Power of Strategic Alignment:
A Guide to Energizing Leadership and Maximizing
Potential in Today's Nonprofit Organizations

Moppin' Floors to CEO:
From Hopelessness and Failure to Happiness and Success

A Guide
to Recruiting
Your Next CEO

The Executive Search Handbook
for Nonprofit Boards

By Dennis C. Miller
with a little help from my good friend,
Michele Hickey

EMERALD LAKE
BOOKS
Sherman, Connecticut

Books published by Emerald Lake Books may be ordered through booksellers or by visiting emeraldlakebooks.com.

ISBN: 978-0-9971207-9-0 (paperback)
        978-1-945847-00-4 (ebook)

Library of Congress Control Number: 2017954252

Dedication

This book is dedicated to the millions of men and women who voluntarily serve on a nonprofit board, committed to creating a positive social impact in the communities they serve, whether locally, nationally or globally.

Contents

Introduction

As a board member of a nonprofit organization, the most important responsibility you are likely to assume will be to hire your chief executive officer. Recent studies have estimated that more than 75% of current nonprofit executives plan to leave their positions in the next five to ten years. For the purpose of our discussion, the terms "chief executive officer," "CEO" or "executive director" will be used synonymously in identifying the top-paid leader of the nonprofit organization.

Two major factors are driving the increased focus on succession planning in the nonprofit sector. First, we are experiencing the expected retirement of a baby boomer generation that sought out careers in the nonprofit sector because of the culture of social change in the 1960s and 1970s. Second, nonprofit boards are realizing the need for executive leaders to possess new leadership competencies to navigate today's rapidly changing environment while successfully leading their organizations into the future.

Traditionally, a passion for the mission along with skill sets ranging from program development, grant writing and community relations were considered sufficient when selecting an executive. This is no longer the case.

Today, nonprofit boards appreciate that the skills required to successfully lead an organization have changed dramatically.

In this book, I will describe the new leadership competencies required to succeed as a social impact leader in the 21st century.

In addition to the new leadership competencies, there also needs to be a cultural fit as well. I will also address the importance of incorporating your organization's values into the recruitment and hiring process.

In my thirty-five years of experience as a board chair, CEO, nonprofit leadership coach and executive search recruiter, I have advised hundreds of organizations on executive leadership development, succession planning, leadership transitions and recruiting chief executives.

My purpose for writing this book is to help prepare the millions of nonprofit board members in our country to address this challenging responsibility.

In *A Guide to Recruiting Your Next CEO*, I will provide answers to many of the questions you may have about how to recruit and hire your next chief executive.

Here are the questions I hear most often:

- Should our organization develop a new strategic plan now or wait for the new CEO to develop such a plan?

- Have we mentored and cultivated the talents of current executive staff members who could "step up" to the CEO role?

- What skills should we look for in our next chief executive?

- Will these skills be the same as or different from those of our current executive?

- How shall we recruit the new executive?

- Should we use an executive search firm?

- Who on the board should participate in the search process?

- How do we involve other members of the executive team?

- What compensation package should be prepared to offer the new candidate?

- How can we use the search process to prepare our board, and our organization, to address the challenges of tomorrow?

This book includes the following chapters:

- Understanding the Search Process
- Defining the Strategic Vision
- Identifying the Right CEO Leadership Competencies and Values
- Activating the Search Committee
- Identifying and Screening Candidates
- Conducting the Interview Process
- Checking References
- Negotiating the Offer
- Onboarding the Candidate

You may want to jump ahead to a particular chapter, but I recommend first reading the book in its entirety. This way, you will gain a much better understanding of the entire executive search process and how to successfully prepare your board for the responsibilities of recruiting your next chief executive officer.

Though the focus of this book is on how to best recruit your next chief executive, many of the same principles will apply if you need to recruit your next chief operating, chief financial or chief development officer.

Our lives are enriched every day by the positive social impact that America's nonprofit sector creates in our communities, whether local, national or global. The need for competent and courageous executive nonprofit leadership has never been greater.

Whether your organization's mission is focused on healthcare, education, arts and culture, children and family services, the environment, professional associations or foundations, it is my hope that this book will support you and your fellow board members as you accept the challenge of recruiting and hiring your next chief executive officer. With knowledge, confidence and teamwork, you will be well on your way to selecting the best CEO to lead your organization forward.

Chapter 1

Understanding the Search Process

*If your actions inspire others to dream more, learn more,
do more and become more, you are a leader.*

John Quincy Adams

Your organization's chief executive officer just announced that she is resigning or retiring from her position. Now what? You relied on her for so much, from human resource management to fundraising. Now what do you do?

Before you embark on this tremendous responsibility, ask yourself these questions:

- Who on our executive team or board has extensive experience with chief executive recruitment?

- Who has the knowledge and insight to identify the required skills and experience the new chief executive officer will need to be effective in this role?

- How likely are we to recruit and persuade candidates who are happy in their current positions to leave their organizations to work for us?

- Who will do the actual work of recruiting, screening and performing initial reviews of candidates?

- What will the ultimate cost be for taking on this task internally, compared with the cost of retaining a search firm?

- Can we use the search process as an opportunity to become a better organization?

As an experienced executive search recruiter for the nonprofit sector, I admit that I am biased against any attempt to recruit your next chief executive on your own. My observation has been that boards who take on the CEO recruitment challenge without professional help are apt to limit their search to applicants who are actively seeking new employment.

While it is, of course, possible to find a qualified CEO this way, you are still working with an incomplete picture of the executive talent available to you. A professional search consultant will expand your candidate pool to include highly motivated, high-performing executives who are not currently in the market for a new position.

The biggest reason given by boards to conduct their search themselves is to avoid the fee for engaging a retained search firm. Retainer search consultants charge a percentage of the chief executive's base salary, usually in the range of 20% to 30%. If your chief executive officer's salary is $200,000 and your search fee is 25%, your expense for conducting the search will be $50,000. However, when you find a successful match, the amortization of this fee over the course of your next chief executive officer's tenure in your organization could be $5,000 per year if they remain in their job for a period of ten years.

I will be the first to say that executive recruiters are not always perfect and they do occasionally misinterpret the quality of a match between CEO and organization. However, unless an experienced executive recruiter serves on your board, it can be a costlier endeavor in the long run to recruit your next chief executive officer on your own. In fact, most organizations seriously underestimate the time and energy that will be required by the board to conduct a search. Combine that with the risk that a poor match will require a repeat search within a year (which most search firms will take on at no additional charge). Your organization will suffer as board and staff energy are funneled away from core activities such as programming, public relations and fundraising. And make no mistake: major individual and institutional donors will become concerned when your organization is operating for an extended period without a chief executive.

Once you have made your decision to perform the search either internally or hire an experienced search firm, I recommend the following process for searching for your next chief executive officer:

1. Identify the strategic challenges the new chief executive officer will be faced with in your organization along with the skills and experience needed to effectively address them. What is your desired future direction? What specific strategic goals and implementation plan needs to be developed to achieve the new vision?

2. Conduct an objective, in-depth assessment of your organization and board governance to determine your strengths and any areas in need of improvement related to best operating and governance practices.

3. Develop a comprehensive customized position and ideal candidate profile for the CEO. This profile will include the specific competencies and experiences you are seeking in your next CEO.

4. Conduct a targeted search into organizations and sectors that align with your organization to identify executives with the relevant skill sets and qualifications required by your organization.

5. Develop a list of qualified prospects for consideration.

6. Approach potential candidates to test their interest in the new position, communicate the strengths of your organization, and persuade strong candidates to consider the new opportunity.

7. Organize a board-level search committee to screen candidates and schedule interviews.

8. Present the most qualified candidates to meet with the search committee after conducting in-depth interviews and reference checks.

9. Select the most qualified candidate and offer them the position.

10. Negotiate a compensation package and other related benefits.

11. Notify all candidates who applied and interviewed for the position and thank them for applying.

12. Provide a plan for onboarding and ongoing support for your new CEO.

Developing the Ideal Position Profile

It is amazing to me how many times I have asked members of the senior team and board to describe the experiences, qualifications and knowledge they wish to have in their next chief executive and they answer, "We want someone just like our current CEO."

Now, I will agree that is a nice endorsement of your current chief executive officer. I am glad to know he or she is well-respected and admired by your organization. But the challenges and opportunities that confronted your former CEO may be very different from those facing your organization today and in the coming years.

Wouldn't it be better to identify the strategic challenges ahead and the new leadership skill sets needed by your next chief executive officer to meet them?

If you would like to see a sample position profile for a new CEO, there is one on my website. You can find it at denniscmiller.com/CEOprofile.

Chapter 2
Defining the Strategic Vision

*Leadership is the capacity
to transform vision into reality.*

Warren G. Bennis

The reality has set in about your need to recruit a new chief executive officer. You know your organization needs someone to oversee the day-to-day operations, to manage the staff, to ensure program goals are met, and to raise funds.

As panic about the pending departure of your CEO gives way to thinking about the future, you will likely begin asking some thought-provoking questions. Is your organization fulfilling its mission to the best of its ability? What is the strategic vision that drives your work? Do all stakeholders share this vision? Are we all working toward it? What is the strategic vision for your nonprofit organization that you want your next leader to achieve?

What Comes First, the Chicken or the Egg?

The good news is, while leadership change is challenging, it is also filled with opportunity. At its best, new executive leadership refreshes an organization, bringing new ideas and energy to its mission-focused work.

The one question I am frequently asked by board chairs is: Should we develop our strategic plan first and then recruit our next CEO, or should we just hire the CEO and leave it up to them to develop the plan?

My answer is to develop your strategic plan first or, at a minimum, identify the key strategic goals your organization will need to achieve to sustain your mission and continue to make a positive difference in the lives of those you serve.

There is a significant downside risk to hiring a new chief executive officer before you engage in at least some self-examination and strategic goal development. You could easily find that you have a newly-hired chief executive who doesn't have the ability see your vision through. Strategic planning prior to hiring gives you the opportunity to match the skill sets of your next chief executive to your board's vision of the organization's future.

For example, what if your organization hires someone with great experience in developing new programs and services, but who has no experience in the world of philanthropy? If, during the strategic planning process, you determine that one of your key strategic goals is creating new donors and new dollars, you will end up with a mismatch between your CEO's strengths and your organization's needs.

Similarly, if it is determined that one of your key strategic challenges is creating a more engaged board but you have already hired a CEO with little or no strong experience in board development, you will be struggling to achieve your organizational goals. Worse, your new CEO may become disheartened when he begins to understand that his skills are inadequate to his new role.

It will be helpful to ask yourselves a few questions about your organization:

- Does your current vision statement still represent a realistic, credible, attractive future for your organization?

- Does it continue to inspire all stakeholders or is it a bit stale?

- What were last year's top achievements?

- How well do you communicate your achievements and successes with all stakeholders, internal and external?

- What do you see as the major internal obstacles to achieving your vision?

- What are your key strategic goals this year?

- How would you measure your organization's success?

- How well is your organization known in the community?

- What makes you distinctive?

- How would you describe the positive social impact you are having?

- How well do you retain current donors?

- How engaged and motivated is your board?

You can decide whether you need to develop a comprehensive strategic plan or if it will be sufficient to just identify the key strategic goals you need your next leader to achieve. But your organization should spend the time and energy for at least some self-examination and vision development.

Strategic Goals

The following areas should be included in your assessment as you work to identify your key strategic goals:

- Mission and Vision
- Organizational Infrastructure
- Fundraising and Development
- Board and CEO Relationship
- Impactful Programs and Services
- Building a Positive Brand

Mission and Vision

Mission answers the questions, "What is your purpose? Why do you exist?" Vision answers the questions, "Where are you going? What is your desired future direction?"

Your vision needs to be a realistic, credible, attractive future for your organization. Your vision should be your articulation of a destination toward which your organization should aim, a future that in many important ways is better, more successful or more desirable than your present.

It should be a signpost pointing the way for all who need to understand where the organization intends to go. Based on my experience, vision statements should set standards of excellence, inspire enthusiasm, encourage commitment, and be well-articulated and easily understood. Above all, your vision should be ambitious and measurable.

Does your organization currently have a vision statement that inspires all of your stakeholders? Will it inspire your next chief executive? Does it have established measures to identify the progress you are making? Is your entire organization strategically aligned to achieve your vision?

Organizational Infrastructure

Will your next chief executive officer have the necessary organizational infrastructure to achieve your vision or will they need to build the structure upon arrival?

Your strategic plan should outline the current management organization chart and identify any potential areas that will need to be enhanced. For example, will it be important for your next CEO be more of an "outside" person developing relationships with key funders, business and community leaders? Or will they need to be an "inside" CEO who will need to focus heavily on internal operational and financial issues?

Do you have the information technology you need to compete effectively? Do you have the staff to perform the new marketing and public relations initiatives you have identified? Are your facilities in need of repair or renovation?

A key component of your strategic plan should include an assessment of your organizational infrastructure, including staff, technology and facility needs.

Fundraising and Development

Every strategic plan requires a resource development plan to ensure the organization's ability to secure the necessary financial resources to sustain your mission. A comprehensive resource or fund development plan should include, at a minimum, the following components:

- A written case for support identifying who you are and the positive social impact you have made, how you will utilize the investments donated from donors to achieve your organization's vision of a better future, and how the donor will benefit by giving to your organization.

- A timeline for ensuring that 100% of the board is providing annual support toward the operating budget. In addition, every member of a board of trustees or directors of an organization should be including that organization among their personal list of top three charities, in terms of financial and time commitment.

- Identification of the top ten potential donors with a cultivation and solicitation strategy for each.

- A diversified plan to include corporate, business and foundation gifts, individual major gift prospects, grants and donor recognition events.

- Creation of a development committee within the board consisting of members willing to work with the leadership team to cultivate prospective donors.

Board and CEO Relationship

Prospective candidates for the CEO position will (and should) ask, "What is the board like?" and you need to be prepared to give an answer.

In my book, *The Nonprofit Board Therapist*, I describe the four documented stages of board governance, which you may find useful:

- A founding board performs all the work of the organization until they can hire paid staff.

- A fiduciary role for the board generally emerges after all staff have been hired. Here, the board sets goals, develops policies, sets direction for the staff, and plays a more passive oversight role.

- As an organization matures, the board can take on a more strategic role and work together with the staff to develop and monitor the strategic and business plans. The board becomes more active in goal setting and achievement.

- The fourth stage of a board's developing role is one of leadership. In this role, the board continues to function in the fiduciary and strategic/business roles, but plans a more active role in partnership with the CEO. In this stage, board governance involves putting forth new ideas, challenging management assumptions, and striving to continually refresh and renew the goals of the organization.

During the search process, it is important to identify at which stage of governance your board is functioning. In my experience, a mature board that is working in a true partnership with the chief executive officer achieves more success. A leadership transition can pave the way for moving from one stage to the next.

The relationship between the board chair and the chief executive officer is crucial. Every CEO needs a supportive board chair, as well as a relationship that has honest and frequent communication, dialogue and feedback for it to be beneficial to the organization. It is also the responsibility of the board chair and the CEO to make sure each board member is fully engaged, with an active role on the board.

Every board member has talents that can be tapped for the benefit of the organization. One board member may be an expert at community outreach; another might be great at social media and communications; yet another board member may have strong financial planning experience. It is a key responsibility for a CEO to actively work with every member of the board in the pursuit of your strategic vision and goals.

How will you describe to your prospective CEO what your board is like? How engaged are they? What are their expectations regarding the new chief executive officer? How will the board evaluate the CEO as part of their annual assessment?

As you consider CEO candidates, consider what their experience is in building relationships with members of their previous board.

Impactful Programs and Services

Regardless of your mission, your programs and services are the core purpose of your organization. They will ultimately determine how much positive social impact you are generating for the community you serve.

A key component of your strategic plan is identifying the following:

- Which programs do you think should be enhanced, developed or terminated?

- Do you have adequate and appropriate tools to evaluate program results to make this determination?

- Do you want to collaborate with other organizations to achieve greater efficiencies and results?

- Would your organization benefit from a merger or strategic affiliation?

Be prepared to address these questions and other similar ones when interviewing prospective candidates to be your next chief executive officer.

Building a Positive Brand

Today, more than ever before, developing a positive brand identity for your nonprofit organization should be a key strategic goal. Brand identity is the total promise your organization makes to clients, employees, board members, donors and volunteers. It is the sum of all your organization does—its mission, vision, values, personality and commitment to those you serve. It is a means of identifying and distinguishing your organization from others.

An organization with a durable, unique brand identity has a strong sense of self-awareness, a motivated team of employees who are proud of their work, active board members and engaged donors.

When interviewing your next chief executive, make sure your discussions include how to move your organization's brand awareness to the next level of success. One of the recurring themes many of my clients voice is the lack of community awareness about their organization and its work. Too often I hear, "We are the best kept secret in town."

Let's continue our discussion with the leadership skills you will seek for your next chief executive officer.

Chapter 3

Identifying the Right CEO Leadership Competencies and Values

To handle yourself, use your head;
to handle others, use your heart.

Eleanor Roosevelt

Whether the board is seeking to replace a retiring executive director or requesting a search for a new CEO to move their organization to greater levels of success, the leadership competencies they are seeking are much different than those of past generations of nonprofit leaders.

As an executive search consultant for the nonprofit sector, I can tell you that boards today are seeking chief executives with transformational leadership styles.

In the past, boards placed a strong emphasis on recruiting executives who were passionate about the mission, experienced with grant writing and program development, and had good management and community relations skills.

Though these skills remain important, the following leadership competencies are taking precedence:

- Visionary thinker
- Entrepreneurial spirit
- Relationship builder
- Emotionally intelligent
- Brand builder
- Collaborator
- Inspirational motivator

Today's leaders need to be visionary thinkers. Nonprofit executives need to chart the future direction for their organizations and communicate it effectively to all stakeholders. Whereas in the past the board may have set the vision, now more boards are asking executives to step forward and fully participate in articulating and realizing the vision. Though board – chief executive dialogue remains crucial to setting an organization's vision, board members want their executive leader to take a prominent role in bringing the vision to life.

Having an entrepreneurial spirit is another key competency required by today's transformational nonprofit leaders. Executive directors need to become the "chief entrepreneurial officer" for their organizations. Whereas in the past executives had to manage an organization's revenue and expenses, today's highly competitive nonprofit environment requires creativity in building a sustainable business model.

In the for-profit world, chief executives are paid for increasing their stock price and improving the net worth of their investors. The nonprofit leaders of today need to be paid for doing something very similar. Your "nonprofit stock price" increases with the positive achievements of your organization. Measurable positive outcomes need to be communicated effectively. Board members need to be engaged as ambassadors promoting your good will. The higher your stock price, the greater the likelihood that people will want to invest in your success.

As a result, a core competency of today's nonprofit leader is the ability to build trusting relationships. Leaders who can bring out the best in others and make people feel their voices, concerns and actions matter are most likely to build successful organizations.

A leader's job is to help their board and staff understand that individual goals are tied into achieving organizational goals. A nonprofit executive who consistently makes decisions that benefit the organization and align with the organization's mission will earn stakeholders' trust, respect and loyalty.

I know from personal experience and the vast amount of available research on emotional intelligence that people who can understand and manage their own and others' emotions make better leaders. Leaders who possess a high level of emotional intelligence recognize and regulate their behavior, embrace open communication and show a greater ability to adapt to different work situations. They are also able to express empathy for others and collaborate more effectively with their executive team members and their boards.

Jack Welch, former chairman of General Electric, was quoted as saying, "No doubt, emotional intelligence is rarer than book smarts, but my experience says it is actually more important in the making of a leader. You just can't ignore it."

Another new core competency for today's transformational nonprofit leaders is the ability to serve as the chief branding officer. The concept of building a positive brand identity for your organization is very important. The chief executive is the face of the organization. Though sometimes the board chair takes on this role, it is increasingly the role of the executive director to be the chief communicator, proudly letting everyone know of the organization's achievements and results (and thereby increasing your stock price).

Traditionally, nonprofit leaders informed stakeholders about the number of programs and services offered, the number of people served or tickets sold, and other organizational statistics. These facts were often viewed as indicators of organizational success. The reality today is that funders and investors are more interested in outcomes and positive results. They want a return on their investment, in terms of real and measurable improvement in the community. Nonprofit leaders need to build an organization's positive brand through constant communication of these achievements and successes.

The ability to work collaboratively is yet another key competency for nonprofit leaders. There was a time when nonprofit leaders emphasized the number of programs they controlled—the more programs they controlled, the greater their empire. The opposite is true today. Success increases when leaders are willing to engage in discussions around collaboration.

In recruiting and rewarding new leaders, boards should be seeking executives whose personality allows them to be more collaborative and less controlling. Funders are seeking ways to foster and increase collaboration and are interested in receiving proposals that involve "teaming up" between organizations to achieve a common goal. Collaborating with a competitor requires a new form of leadership thinking.

Finally, today's nonprofit leaders need to be inspirational, able to motivate their staffs, board, donors and key stakeholders. An organization's success often rests on a shared sense of passion and on a collective pursuit of excellence at every level of the organization. Leaders who listen and actively seek input from their staff and board increase morale. They make decisions that are consistent with the organization's values and that promote the good of the organization. They earn the trust and respect of others. They set high expectations of themselves and for their staff and board, communicate these expectations, and hold people accountable. More importantly, they create a winning attitude that conveys the message that their organization is "the place to be."

Inspiring and motivating others toward achievement of a common vision, having an entrepreneurial spirit, building trusting and respectful relationships, proudly communicating your organization's achievements, and seeking collaboration are all skills required and sought after for today's nonprofit transformational leadership. Only those leaders who can demonstrate the three Cs—courage, confidence and competence—need apply.

When searching for your next chief executive officer, make sure you identify the key leadership competencies in each of your prospective candidates that best match your organization's strategic needs.

In addition to possessing the new leadership competencies required to be a successful chief executive officer in the nonprofit sector, a candidate's values and their ability to be a "cultural fit" are equally important. An organization that clearly defines its values and lives by them will see happier employees, increased donors and a stronger board commitment to achieve its strategic vision and goals.

An organization that is not clear about its core values, or that struggles to stand by them, will likewise struggle with engaging stakeholders and building a positive brand identity. If this describes your organization, I advise you to address the matter immediately, before you begin your search process. If you don't know what you stand for, how will you know what values to look for in your candidates? Core values are more than a tagline. They are infused throughout your entire work culture. New employees, particularly those at the executive level, must understand and contribute to fulfilling these values.

Therefore, it is critically important to communicate your organization's core values to candidates early in the recruiting process. Doing so will let candidates know what you stand for and will help them to determine whether they will fit comfortably into your work culture. Those who are impressed and excited about the opportunity to work in your organization will continue to pursue the position. Those who perceive a poor fit will self-select to withdraw their candidacy.

When you incorporate your organization's values into your recruitment process, your new chief executive officer will quickly align with your culture and be a happier and more productive leader. They will be more engaged and motivated, and will be positioned to inspire morale throughout your organization.

The role of a search committee and its chair is next up for discussion.

Chapter 4

Activating the Search Committee

*Our chief want is someone who will inspire us
to be what we know we could be.*

Ralph Waldo Emerson

Every nonprofit organization needs an effective leader to
sustain its mission so that it can make a positive difference in
the lives of those it serves. Finding individuals who possess
the qualifications and experience needed to strategically align
your organization to achieve its vision *and who are well-suited
to your nonprofit's culture* will be challenging. A well-organized
search committee to oversee the recruitment process of your
next CEO will add tremendous value to the process.

The main purpose of the search committee is to develop
a process to recruit, screen and interview candidates. The
committee then recommends a list of final candidates to
the full board.

Depending upon the size and structure of your board,
the ideal size for a search committee is five to seven members,
including the committee chair. The availability and experience
of those serving on your board will also play a role in your
committee's size. Members of the committee must be willing

to invest their time and talents throughout the entire search process, which can take many months.

In addition to key decision makers and highly respected members of the board, the search committee may want to include a non-board volunteer with extensive experience in nonprofit organizations, leadership development or search experience. If you decide to conduct the search without the guidance and experience of a search firm, you may still want to consider hiring a search consultant to serve on your committee. Your current or incoming board chair should also be part of the committee.

An effective search requires balancing the long-term strategic planning needs of the organization with the urgency to recruit the right candidate. The search committee should develop an efficient process from start to finish. As a first step, committee members should begin to quietly reach out to business colleagues, board members and other constituents who may lead them to qualified candidates.

While this initial networking is progressing, the committee should begin to address the following questions:

- Does everyone agree on the required competencies and expectations of the next chief executive officer?

- Has the entire committee agreed upon your organization's strategic vision?

- Have you decided on whether you are going to retain an executive search firm?

- Do you know what salary and benefit package you will offer as part of the new CEO's compensation?

- How will you publicly announce you are conducting a search?

- How often do you plan to meet?

- Do you know how many candidates the committee will want to interview?

- Have you agreed upon a timeframe for making an offer and a start date for the next CEO?

- Have you developed a consensus on your process and how you will keep the full board involved?

It is crucial that all members of the committee agree to protect the confidentiality of potential applicants. If a candidate's current employer found out that one of their key staff was interviewing for a new position, it could jeopardize the current employment of the candidate or, worse yet, subject your organization to potential litigation. Your organization's image and reputation in the professional community could also be damaged.

The next key step is to appoint a search committee chair. The ideal search committee chair will be a highly respected and trusted member of the board. They need to have strong leadership and communication skills and be a consensus builder. The chair will keep everyone on the committee and the entire board fully apprised of any updates on the search process.

The chair must also be a good listener and collaborator ensuring that all members of the committee are given an opportunity to voice their opinions. It is important that the chair control the flow of discussion and not allow any one member to dominate the conversation.

The major responsibilities of the search committee chair are to:

- Communicate to the full board of trustees, especially the board chair, throughout the entire process.

- Recruit and select members of the committee.

- Establish a committee structure and provide leadership to the committee.

- Develop the agenda and timelines for the search process.

- Create a system for recruiting, interviewing, screening and selecting candidates.

- Ensure reference checking is completed and terms of the compensation offer have been approved.

- Make sure that all final candidates who were not selected for the chief executive officer position are contacted and thanked for their participation.

- Develop a transition plan for the newly appointed CEO.

The chair must ensure that all members of the search committee have agreed to the vision or future direction of the organization and the Ideal Position Profile for the CEO. (If your position profile still needs work, can find a sample for inspiration at denniscmiller.com/CEOprofile.)

The search committee chair organizes the committee, drives the process and schedules the meeting dates and timelines for making key decisions. When recommending the final candidates to the full board, the chair also ensures that consensus is achieved.

Occasionally, I am asked if I think a former board chair would be appropriate to chair the search committee. The answer is maybe. If this former chair is a forward-thinking leader who knows the strategic goals of your organization and is not married to the past, it could work. Many times, however, a former chair is not as involved in knowing your new vision and current strategic goals to lead the process effectively.

Another important question I am very frequently asked is whether the current CEO or founder or members of the senior management team should serve on the search committee. My immediate answer is *absolutely not*! In my experience, your retiring (or otherwise exiting) chief executive officer should not be involved in selecting the next CEO.

He should, however, be asked for input in creating the Ideal Position Profile, as his experience can provide valuable input into the knowledge, experience and qualifications needed for the position. He knows the job better than anyone serving on the committee and may have something valuable to offer in terms of envisioning the future of the organization.

That's where his involvement should end. To have him at the table when reviewing candidates or during the interview process will dampen the committee's ability to move in a new direction.

In fact, I have seen far too often that the presence of the current CEO as a member of the search committee creates bias in the search process. They hamper open and free discussion regarding the skills needed to move your organization forward.

I have a colleague who was an internal candidate for the retiring CEO position, who was serving on the search committee. In an interview, with her CEO present, she was asked what changes she would make to the organization.

Did you really think she was going to open up and "spill the beans" on the current CEO's shortcomings?

In another situation, the founder convinced the selected final candidate not to take the job. It was determined she really wanted her daughter, who worked in the organization, to get the job.

It is also not wise to add senior members of the management team to the search committee. They should not be selecting their next boss. It is completely appropriate, and even advised, to have them interview, either individually or as a group, the final candidates selected by the search committee. Their input is important, but the board should make the final decision.

After selecting the search committee chair, one of the key decisions your committee will need to make is whether to hire an experienced outside search firm. It is amazing how many professionals I know who serve on a nonprofit board who have said that their biggest mistake was thinking they could recruit their next chief executive on their own.

Retaining an executive search firm can dramatically reduce the time commitment required by each committee member. The firm will oversee the identification and recruitment of prospective candidates, guide the committee through the search process from start to finish, conduct reference checks and ensure that the committee has been engaged in a rigorous and efficient search process.

Should you decide to retain an executive search firm to help lead and provide counsel throughout this process, the search committee will need to develop a written request for proposals (RFP). The committee will then invite a short list of firms to respond to your RFP. As you review proposals, make sure you check references thoroughly. Find out who will be the actual client engagement partner working directly with your chair and search committee. You do not want your search to be handed off to a junior level consultant. While this individual might be qualified to conduct candidate research and reference checking, your search firm's senior partner should be in constant communication with your search committee chair.

Once an executive search firm is selected, the search committee chair and the managing director of the firm will need to maintain and develop a very close working relationship. The search committee chair and the firm will develop a partnership to accomplish the following:

- Schedule timeframes for updates and committee meetings.

- Maintain close day-to-day communication via email and phone.

- Develop the agendas for committee meetings.

- Prepare the committee for its roles and responsibilities.

- Determine the number of candidates and outline the interview process.

- Finalize the search and communicate the offer to the selected candidate.

One final comment on an overlooked role of the search committee is the need to "sell" the candidates on why joining your organization is a great opportunity. Too many times, committees think, *Why don't they see how great we are?*, and they fail to leave a positive impression about themselves or their organization. It is crucial to express to candidates the importance of your organization's mission, its achievements and how proud you are to be serving on its board.

It is just as important for you to make a good impression on candidates as it is for them to impress you. Good candidates invest significant time in seeking advice, researching organizations, practicing interview skills, and preparing their presentations. Search committees should put the same amount of effort into preparing to meet, and impress, candidates. Remember—the top-flight candidates you are interviewing may be discussing positions with other organizations as well. It's easy to forget that the interview process is a two-way street.

Let's turn our attention now to conducting candidate identification and screening.

Chapter 5

Identifying and Screening Candidates

As we look ahead into the next century,
leaders will be those who empower others.

Bill Gates

Now that your search committee has been organized and the competencies and experience required for your next chief executive officer has been agreed upon, you will need to turn your attention to identifying and screening potential candidates. In the past, perhaps the first thing your organization would do is place an ad in the local or regional newspaper and wait for resumes and cover letters to arrive.

Today, with so many online job search sites and career- and industry-related social media platforms, you can develop an efficient strategy for reaching many potential candidates. The more important question, however, is whether these platforms will help you reach the *right* candidates.

Whatever method you choose to advertise a job opening, remember that you're only going to reach individuals who are actively seeking a new position. You might get lucky and find the perfect candidate this way, but consider this: the perfect candidate might not even be thinking all that much about finding a new position. She is not reviewing those job boards and social media feeds, which means your ads and posts are not reaching her.

Why would you want to leave good candidates out of your recruitment effort?

Advertising and plugging away via social media are insufficient alone. A stronger, more comprehensive search includes outreach to passive candidates—professionals who are not currently pursuing a new job. With a little savvy research and old-fashioned hard work, you can build a better slate of candidates.

First, establish a list of target organizations that have some similarities to yours. For example, if you are searching for a museum CEO, you may want to focus on visual arts organizations, historical societies, libraries, educational organizations and the like. Professional associations (in this case, perhaps the American Alliance of Museums and The Association of Academic Museums & Galleries) may have a list you can use, especially if your organization is a member. Guidestar.org is another excellent resource for identifying nonprofit organizations, even at the free subscription level.

As you build your list, consider location. Is your organization likely to attract a prospective CEO candidate from another state who would need to relocate? Would you be willing to pay for her relocation expenses? Some organizations can attract candidates from across the country because of their national reputation. If that is not likely for your organization, then set a reasonable geographic limit to your searches.

Once you've built a list of 50 or so target organizations, look up their executives. If you chose to conduct your search internally, you might want to distribute the list of targeted organizations to members of your search committee for follow-up calls to each organization. Fortunately, most nonprofits have websites that include this information. LinkedIn searches can be useful here as well. Try to get a sense of the hierarchy, and consider the size and scope of the organizations on your list.

Guidestar.org posts the IRS Form 990 for every nonprofit organization in the country. This means you can get a general sense of each organization's budget and what their compensation looks like since each return must list the top five salaries paid that year. Although the returns available on guidestar.org may be a year or two old, you can still get a good idea of the salary range, and this is important.

This information will help take you from a grouping of organizations to a list of potential candidates. For example, suppose your museum has an annual budget of $10 million. You can see that CEOs at smaller organizations are making less than what you can offer, which is great. These CEOs might be viable candidates for your search. On the other hand, you've also looked at organizations with budgets of $50 million or more, and you know you can't match the salaries of their CEOs. However, given that these organizations have larger operations, perhaps there is another C-suite executive on their staff who would be interested in being considered for the position of chief executive officer.

If your search committee decides to conduct the search without the help of an outside firm, make sure your committee members have the time to do this grunt work. The search committee chair will assign duties to committee members about contacting potential candidates on the phone.

If you hire an outside search firm, on the other hand, they will begin to pick up the phone and get to know people.

At one point or another, you've probably gotten a call from a recruiter—"I'm recruiting for a director-level position at XYZ. Do you know of anyone who might be interested? Please feel free to pass this information along."

Yes, it's a bit of a grind, but that's how you find passive candidates. The good news is that most people you contact will try to be genuinely helpful, even if they do not want to put their hat in the ring. Everyone loves to help someone find a great new job!

Our firm has developed extensive contacts at the board and executive team level because of decades of work in the national nonprofit industry. Most search firms also have extensive research capabilities to develop name generation or talent mapping. After they have a significant number of high-potential executives listed, usually 100 plus, executive search consultants and researchers will begin screening the potential targets and determining whether they are suitable candidates.

Resume Screening

Prior to commencing the interview process, your search firm or organization will need to develop an efficient screening process to eliminate those candidates who lack the desired competencies and skills required by your next CEO.

Having hired and recruited hundreds of professionals, I have developed a very useful series of screening steps that have helped me successfully weed through applications over the years.

In instances when a candidate has been recommended to me, the first thing I do is consider my relationship and experience with the person who made the recommendation. Do I trust and respect their knowledge and perception of talent? Have they recommended candidates to me in the past who have succeeded in their new job? What is their personal connection to the candidate and what insights can they provide?

The second step is to review resumes of candidates, sorting them into three categories:

- **Yes.** Their resume looks terrific and their professional experience appears to be a very close match to our ideal profile. They will be selected for the first round of interviews.

- **Maybe.** Their resumes have many of the qualifications and experiences my client or organization is seeking, but there are aspects of their professional background that don't look like a solid match.

- **Not interested.** It is amazing to me how many people with no experience related to the qualifications and background needed for the job apply for it regardless. It looks like they send out resumes to all job postings and hope something sticks. They will receive a nice thank you letter informing them that other candidates more closely match the needs of our client.

Over the past thirty-five years, I have developed an instinct for reviewing resumes that has helped me classify resumes into one of the three above categories. First, I ask myself the following type of questions:

- Does the resume immediately grab my attention?

- Is the candidate's name and contact information easy to find?

- Are the candidate's professional work history and quantifiable achievements clearly listed?

- Is the resume well-formatted or does it use some "creative" resume writing style that makes it difficult to parse the facts of the candidate's work history? For example, is there a full-page list of functional qualifications that neglects to list the name of the candidate's last employer and dates of employment?

- Are there obvious spelling and grammatical mistakes?

Today, many human resource professionals accept both the chronological and functional resume. Call me old-fashioned, but I prefer the chronological style. I like to learn the candidate's track record of employment, promotion and tenure. When I see that the person has had five jobs in two years or less, or has been in their current position for less than a year, the resume goes immediately into my "not interested" pile. Granted, there may be extenuating circumstances, but it is an immediate red flag to me and it should be to you as well.

I am looking for achievements and results for my clients. The resume that lists the responsibilities for each job while not providing a specific achievement or positive result does not stimulate my interest.

In regard to time-gaps on a resume, I don't believe that all gaps are negative. For example, recently I was asked by a colleague if I would meet with a woman who was seeking advice on how to find a new position. The woman was concerned about the gaps in her resume because she had been out of work for a few years. She did have a prior positive work history and had been steadily promoted in her career. But like many women, she decided to stay home to raise her children. She went on to tell me that she had gone through a difficult divorce and needed to work. She was concerned that the gap in her employment was going to be a red flag to a prospective employer.

I told her to list on her resume that she earned a PhD in motherhood and to be proud of her decisions. I encouraged her to accept herself and to be honest when she has an opportunity for an interview. She called me the following month to share the good news that she applied for a position she was clearly qualified for and won the job.

Assessment Tools

Many organizations have begun using assessment tools to determine if candidates are a good cultural fit. In fact, assessment tools have become a fast-growing segment of the HR technology market. These tools can measure personality traits and a candidate's emotional intelligence. Both are important factors in the hiring of an organization's chief executive officer. I have experience working with employee assessment and talent development tools, and often include them when I am conducting the executive search process.

Advocates for assessment tools argue that their tests can help identify what motivates job candidates and, as a result, they help lead to better hiring decisions. The value of these tools is their ability to determine how a candidate will interact with others on the job and how they approach problem solving.

Assessments provide insights into other performance-related issues as well. For example, an important characteristic of a leader is how they will work with everyone in the organization, from top to bottom.

The important thing, however, is to remember that the assessment tool is only one component of the search process, not an end to itself. Assessment tools can predict certain behaviors, but personal interviews will enable you to get a much better understanding of whether the candidate will be a good match for your organization. Therefore, phone and face-to-face interviews should remain a very important component of the search process for recruiting your next chief executive officer. How does the candidate interact with members of the search committee? With members of your senior management team?

Phone Interviews

Telephone interviews offer an efficient, and surprisingly effective, screening tool prior to the face-to-face interviews. An initial phone conversation can yield valuable information about a candidate's motivation for seeking the position, whether their current compensation is aligned with yours, their ability to listen, and what their expectations are about the new position.

The phone interview is a low-cost alternative for conducting the first round of interviews. It is an easy way to screen candidates whose resumes appear to be a good match to your ideal position profile. In my experience, an initial phone interview should last about 15 to 30 minutes. The following is a list of sample questions you might want to ask:

- Why are you interested in this position now?

- What has been your greatest career achievement?

- How would you describe your leadership style?

- How would others describe you?

- What is your current compensation?

- What are your salary expectations?

There have been several HR business articles that address the value of asking candidates for their salary history. Asking about salary history is a good way to eliminate candidates who are already earning above the amount you are willing or able to offer. However, there is a growing concern from some that once the candidate reveals their salary, you will adjust your offer to their current/past salary level. From my experience, the main reason employers request this information is to gauge how likely a candidate is to accept an offer the company is prepared to make. However, in 2017, New York City passed a law banning the salary history question. Therefore, check your state and local laws to be sure it is permissible to ask about prior salary if this is a question you want to include in interviews.

You will most likely learn within a relatively short period of time whether to schedule a face-to-face interview or decide that you are not interested in expressing further interest in the candidate.

Let's turn our discussion to the interview process.

Chapter 6

Conducting the Interview Process

*Continuous effort, not strength or intelligence,
is the key to unlocking our potential.*

Sir Winston Churchill

Congratulations! The hard work of your search committee has generated a list of viable candidates to interview to become your next chief executive officer. It's time to schedule face-to-face interviews with the candidates. Contact them to let them know the times, dates and locations of the interviews. It is best to provide a few dates and times to accommodate their schedule, if possible.

Any responsible and ethical search firm should have interviewed all viable candidates in person before they recommend your search committee meet with them. I find it remarkable how many times people have told me they never met in person with the search firm that recruited them prior to meeting with members of the hiring organization's search committee. There is no way a candidate for the chief executive officer position of your organization should meet with members of your search committee without first being screened in person by a senior executive member of the firm.

It is appropriate today to use services such as Skype early in the interview process, but to present candidates to a search committee without ever first meeting them in person is completely unprofessional in my opinion. If you are still considering whether to hire an outside search firm, make sure you have an answer as to whether they interview final candidates in person. This "extra touch" separates the quality firms from the rest.

The following are several recommendations for conducting interviews with your final candidates:

- Ask the same initial questions to all candidates to ensure a fair comparison of candidates.

- Consider developing a final candidate evaluation matrix or scoring system for each candidate to compare the result of all interviews. You can download a sample matrix from my website at denniscmiller.com/candidatescore that can be modified for your specific needs.

- All questions should be limited to the performance of duties as required by your next CEO. Do not ask questions about race, nationality, gender, birth date, spouse, disabilities or children.

- Ask open-ended questions and avoid questions that require a "yes" or "no" answer.

- Ask some thought-provoking and challenging questions. (See the samples later in this chapter.) Remember, you are trying to determine if this candidate has the ability to handle the job as your CEO.

- Make sure you are listening, not just talking. Don't let silence make you uncomfortable or anxious. The more you talk, the less time you have to learn about the candidate.

You should note that federal law does not prohibit employers from asking about a candidate's criminal history. But, federal Equal Employment Opportunity laws do prohibit employers from discriminating based upon criminal history information. Check the laws in your state too, though, since a number have passed laws prohibiting requesting information on prior criminal history.

Another question is whether it is legal to ask a candidate about their credit history. A few states and the federal government have begun to consider the legality of such a practice. Therefore, you will want to check your state law on this issue as well. For example, some states have passed laws requiring an employer to have a valid basis for asking to review a credit score as it relates to the responsibilities of the position. However, if you decide to proceed with these questions, it is best to get the candidate's written permission.

The interview process should be a two-way exploration to determine if the candidate is a good fit for your organization and whether your organization is a good fit for them. Candidates should also come prepared to ask you questions about your organization. As a former board chair and CEO, I have always found great value in candidates' more probing and challenging questions about our organization.

I am often asked how many candidates the search committee should interview. The answer depends upon the committee's time and preference. One client told me they only wanted to interview the final four candidates. Another client wanted to meet everyone I thought was a serious candidate for the position.

At universities and colleges, there are many levels of interviews required prior to approving the final candidate. Final candidates usually meet with members of the faculty and administration as well as members of the search committee. In the healthcare sector, candidates often need to meet with members of a physician medical executive committee and senior management.

It is best for the chair of your search committee and the senior partner of your search firm to be in daily communication on each potential candidate to decide on how many candidates the search committee will interview. There is no absolute number. If I had to err, I would rather interview more than fewer candidates.

When evaluating final candidates, I am most interested in three key aspects:

- How well do they deal with people?

- Do they have a track record of motivating and leading a team to achievement and success?

- How well will the candidate mesh with the culture of the organization?

It is my main responsibility as an executive search consultant to recruit candidates who will effectively lead my client's team, motivate them and integrate with their culture. No matter how accomplished a candidate, no matter how knowledgeable about nonprofit organizations, if they can't motivate and integrate into your organization's culture, they will not lead you to success.

When you are interviewing executive-level candidates for your organization, consider the following:

- **Interpersonal skills.** Good interpersonal skills (such as communication, problem solving and conflict resolution) are vital to success in management. Leaders must understand how to effectively deal with other people.

- **Ability to deliver positive results.** Strong executives have a track record of success (for example, leading teams that increase revenue streams, streamline processes, cut expenses and achieve organizational goals). Their capabilities have already been demonstrated with previous employers.

From my experience, I know some management candidates can sell themselves so well during the interview that it's a surprise when they fail to thrive on the job. You can minimize the likelihood of this happening when you keep the above attributes in mind during the interview and ask questions that enable you to screen for them.

The following are a list of potential questions you may want to use as a guideline in interviewing candidates for the position of CEO for your organization:

- Briefly describe why you are interested in seeking the position of CEO at our organization?

- What qualifications and experiences in your professional background do you feel most qualify you for this position?

- What qualities do you think are required today of a successful leader?

- Based on what you have learned about our organization, what areas of expertise do you feel you might need to hire for, to complement your own?

- What do you think are the two or three key challenges facing our organization today and what would you do as the CEO to address them?

- Tell us about a time when you and your team faced challenging odds. How did you keep them engaged and motivated to overcome the situation and succeed?

- Can you describe a time when you felt challenged ethically at work? What was the situation and how did you handle it?

- Did you see our organization's values posted on our website? What values made an impression on you and why?

- Describe a time when you had to promote an idea or project to a group. How did you go about persuading them?

- In your last position, what was your strategy for building relationships with your team members and peers?

- Relate your experience with building relationships with members of the board.

- What role do you expect your board members to play in our organization?

- Can you provide an example of how you built self-confidence in others that worked for you directly?

- How would you describe your communication style to all stakeholders, internal and external?

- Do you believe it is important to provide mentorships to fellow emerging leaders in your organization? If yes, how have you succeeded at this in the past?

- Who were some of your mentors and how did they help you grow as a leader?

- What professional accomplishment are you most proud of? Why?

- What is your biggest career disappointment? Why?

- Do you agree that the term "nonprofit" refers to our tax status and not our business plan? Why?

- Tell us about a time when you found it necessary to challenge the status quo. What did you do? What was the result?

- What evidence do you have that you have created a positive climate or culture at your current employer?

- What success have you had with increasing donors and dollars with your prior organizations?

- How would you expect to measure the impact of our programs and services under your leadership?

- What are your thoughts about collaborating or merging with other similar mission-based organizations? Have you had any experience with this?

- Tell me about someone from any of your previous employers with whom you found it difficult to get along. What did you do to build a stronger relationship? What was the result?

One note of caution—do not try to ask all these questions in your interview. You do not want to overwhelm or even scare away the candidate. Some of the questions above are intended to learn about experience and expertise. Others are intended to gauge their emotional intelligence.

Select several questions you are comfortable with. My suggestion is to make 20–30% of your questions about emotional intelligence and use the remainder to focus on experience and leadership expertise.

Let the candidates know your approximate timeframe for arriving at a final decision and thank them for meeting with you. If you have not already done so, it is time to perform a thorough check of their references. Let's turn to this subject now.

Chapter 7

Checking References

You can do what I cannot do.
I can do what you cannot do.
Together we can do great things.

Mother Teresa

One of the most important steps in the search process is conducting reference checks on all final candidates. From my experience, there is no better way to gauge past performance than to speak to people who have direct knowledge and experience with their performance.

It is scary to think of the number of search committees who spend five to ten minutes on a phone call with a single reference provided by the candidate and then recommend the candidate for hire without any further scrutiny. On the other hand, some organizations will go the opposite extreme and request ten or more references.

You Can't Make This Stuff Up

In the late 1980s, I was interviewing two final candidates to become the executive director of a medical center's foundation. One candidate was an older man with many years of experience and another was a younger woman with less experience but with obvious potential for great success. At the time, since I was only in my 30s myself, I thought it might be best to bring in the more experienced candidate rather than the one who seemed to have the most potential for tomorrow.

The more senior candidate provided me with a list of ten references. I don't recall asking for that many but I started to call them one at a time. The first six or seven references told me he pretty much walked on water. Working for a Catholic hospital, I thought that was a good quality. I don't know why, but I decided to keep calling. On my eighth call, something seemed off. I remember asking the individual, "Are you telling me that you would be uncomfortable providing a positive reference for this person?" The reply was, "Yes, I would not be comfortable making a positive reference." Now I was curious, so I called references nine and ten. The ninth told me that he was shocked his name was provided as a reference and would never hire the guy again. The tenth told me to do everything in my power not to hire him.

In all my years as a CEO, leadership coach and executive search recruiter, I have never forgotten that memory of speaking to all ten references. The younger candidate, the one I thought had potential from the beginning, was hired and did a fantastic job.

In another situation, our medical center was recruiting a manager for marketing and special event projects and my vice president for marketing came into my office raving about a particular candidate. He felt so strongly about him that he wanted to be able to hire him that day. I reminded the vice president that our policy for hiring included a more comprehensive list of interviews and reference checks. I offered my own time to interview the candidate and then sent him to our human resources department to complete an application and to learn more about our employee benefits prior to contacting his references.

I remember this polished young man showing me his portfolio of marketing projects and telling me he already had two job offers from our competitors. He was hoping to receive an offer from us before he left to go back to Maryland where he lived. I was impressed with his resume and qualifications, but there was something about his personality that made me uncomfortable. I asked him for a list of references.

I called the first name on his list, which happened to be someone from his current employer. I remember asking the person if she could describe for me his level of achievements and related work performance. She told me that her office was next to his but that he reported directly to the CEO. I called the CEO's office and informed her that I was calling about a candidate who was applying for a position with our medical center. I did tell the CEO that I felt a bit uncomfortable with this candidate after I had interviewed him, but wanted to give him the benefit of the doubt and asked if she could provide any feedback on his performance.

Her exact words to me were, "Is this CEO to CEO"? I assured her it was. She then told me that she had never fired anyone in her twenty years of being the CEO, but last week he was the first person she ever fired. I thanked her and hung up. Boy, was I glad I was persistent in getting honest feedback about his job performance.

There is no better way to gauge the potential performance of any candidate than to speak to those who know and have worked with the candidate directly.

Reference checking is crucial to ensuring you are hiring the most qualified person to be your next chief executive officer, and that they will be a good match for your organization. There are candidates who present well during the interview but who may not really be able perform the job duties to your satisfaction. It's even possible to become a "master interviewee" with the help of coaching or plenty of practice.

There is no set number of reference names to contact. A common mistake many organizations make is asking candidates to choose their own references. You will gain more insights into the candidate's skills, abilities and knowledge from someone who has observed the candidate perform. I would request they provide you with a list of references that includes:

- A former board chair or two.

- Former board members who know the candidate well.

- A few senior management team members who worked directly for the candidate.

- Other key stakeholders who know them well on a professional level, including trade association CEOs.

During the interview process, make sure you get written consent from the candidate to call their references. You will need to respect the candidate's wish to keep their current employer from knowing they are looking for a new job. However, this does not prevent you from working behind the scenes to find out who really knows this candidate well. All questions should be job-related. Check with your local and state laws for any specific exclusions.

In today's litigious world, most employers will only provide basic information, such as dates of employment and title. Many organizations are hesitant to provide any more background on the candidate, fearing that the candidate may file a lawsuit if they are turned down for the job. One non-threatening way to address this issue is to assure the individual providing the reference that any information they offer will be kept in strictest confidence. This may help break the ice for a more honest discussion. Your candidate should also inform all references that you will be contacting them prior to your call. This is a must!

How to Conduct the Reference Check

The following are four guidelines for conducting reference checks:

- Provide the reference with your name and title or relationship to your organization, and explain that you are calling about a candidate you are considering for the position of chief executive officer.

- Inquire whether now is convenient for the person to speak with you about the candidate. If not, request to schedule a more appropriate time to call.

- Let the person know you have consent from the candidate to speak to them and that all responses will be kept in strict confidence.

- Allow ample time for the person to answer your questions. Listen and take notes.

The following are some questions you may want to ask the person listed as a reference:

- What were the approximate dates of employment with your organization?

- What was your relationship with the candidate? Board member? CEO? Senior management team?

- How would you describe the candidate's achievements at your organization?

- What set of unique skills did the candidate bring to your organization?

- How would you describe the candidate's social skills and emotional intelligence, especially as related to motivational skills and team building?

- How did others in your organization (for example, board members, etc.) perceive the candidate?

- What were the candidate's greatest strengths?

- What areas were most in need of improvement?

- Considering that we are seeking to hire our next CEO, do you think the candidate would perform well in their duties?

- Would you rehire the candidate? Why or why not?

- Are there any issues, qualities or characteristics about this candidate that we did not discuss that you think it are important for us to know about?

You may want to create a second matrix or scoring system similar to the one you had for scoring the candidates during the interview process. However, this one would be for performing your reference checks and would help you compare the results of the feedback you get. If you'd like, you can download a sample matrix from my website at denniscmiller.com/references.

Educational Credentials

In addition to employment history and job performance, it is crucial that you confirm any college, university or other agency credentials listed on a final candidate's resume.

It isn't as unusual as you might think for a candidate to attempt to inflate, or even fabricate, their educational accomplishments. The best and most effective way to do this is to contact the registrar's office at each college. Provide their name and Social Security information and they can often verify on the spot.

Under the federal Family Educational Rights and Privacy Act (FERPA), graduation or degree verification may be provided by a school since it is considered "directory information."

Even the Nation's Best Organizations Make a Mistake

Five days after naming George O'Leary its new head football coach, the University of Notre Dame announced back in 2001 that O'Leary had resigned suddenly after admitting to falsifying parts of his academic and athletic background.

For two decades, O'Leary, 55, formerly the coach at Georgia Tech, exaggerated his accomplishments as a football player at the University of New Hampshire and falsely claimed to have earned a master's degree in education from New York University. Those misstatements followed him on biographical documents from one coaching position to another until finally reaching Notre Dame, one of the most coveted and scrutinized jobs in college football.

O'Leary's undoing and the university's humiliation took place in a matter of days, beginning with a series of telephone calls placed by a newspaper writing a feature article on O'Leary. It was discovered that former coaches and players at the University of New Hampshire could not remember O'Leary playing there, even though biographical information in various media guides of teams he later coached claimed he had earned varsity letters there from 1966 to 1968.

When Notre Dame officials contacted O'Leary, he admitted the inaccuracies first about his playing career, then about the master's degree. Both he and university officials agreed he should resign and, in a span of 36 hours, O'Leary tumbled from the high point of his career.

A final note on reference checks. Remember that it is up to your organization to be informed about your candidate, especially since they may be hired as your next CEO. Take your time to conduct reference checks before making the offer. Though they may be time-consuming, this is a smart investment of your time. A great hire can lead your organization to new heights of achievement. A bad hire can set you back for years.

Now that your candidate has passed the reference check process, let's turn our attention to making and negotiating the job offer.

Chapter 8

Negotiating the Offer

*If you are successful, it is because somewhere,
sometime, someone gave you a life or an idea
that started you in the right direction.*

Melinda Gates

The light at the end of the tunnel has finally arrived. After all the candidate research, screening and intensive interviewing, your search committee is ready to recommend your final candidate to the full board for approval. You now turn to the subject of compensation. What salary level and benefits is the candidate seeking and what are you prepared to offer?

Presenting and negotiating a job offer with the ideal candidate can be intimidating even for the most experienced person. Negotiating is more of an art than a skill. However, there are a few positive steps you can take to enhance your negotiating ability and land your new CEO.

I highly recommend you let your candidates know the salary range and compensation package that will be offered before you select your final candidates. You want to make sure that a candidate's salary expectations are realistic and in line with your budget. Before you make an offer, it is crucial that you have done your homework on what the market range for a CEO is in your area.

During one recent CEO search, we met a candidate who had a very impressive resume and background, but when she told us her current salary was $350,000—and the hiring organization's budget was approximately $175,000 for this position—we immediately informed her that it would not make sense to formally schedule an interview with her.

There are several compensation studies for the nonprofit sector that can be obtained on the internet. Fees or subscriptions may be required to access them. You can also contact your organization's trade association to determine what the range is for chief executive officers at other organizations similar to yours.

As noted in Chapter 5, every nonprofit organization must submit an annual IRS Form 990 report and they are available on guidestar.org. The data is usually a year or two old, but you can still get a sense of what similar organizations have been paying their top executives. Be sure to take revenue size into account as you compare salary levels. A nonprofit organization with an annual budget of $5 million will pay their CEO much less than one with a $200 million budget.

Regardless of how impressive the candidate is that you are about to make an offer to, every organization has financial limits. In addition to determining the range of salary your organization can offer, build an attractive compensation package that includes a potential annual bonus, retirement plans and any further benefits, including vacation time and holidays. Other perks can include a sign-on bonus, car allowance or a moving allowance for candidates who will be relocating.

I recommend presenting your best offer to a final candidate up front while leaving some room for negotiations. Don't try to "low-ball" your candidate and play games. It will not create a positive start to your relationship.

That said, be aware that your candidate may negotiate a higher starting salary. Negotiation is a two-way street. Listen to their request and consider what flexibility you have. If your initial offer really is the best your organization can do, you will need to let the candidate know that you must stand firm on your offer. Your potential CEO should respect your situation.

Explore other, budget-friendly ways to make the offer more attractive. Perhaps you can add an extra week of vacation or consider an adjustment after the first six months' performance. The negotiation process is an opportunity to let your final candidate know you are excited to have them join your organization.

When I am engaged as a search consultant, I often negotiate the compensation package with the final candidate on behalf of my client. However, occasionally a client will prefer to make the offer themselves, arranging a special meeting with the search committee chair or board chair. There is no fixed rule.

Recently, our firm completed an executive search for a new CEO with a well-known international healthcare foundation. After the final candidate was offered the job along with the salary and benefit package approved by my client, the board chair met with the new CEO in person and decided to sweeten the deal to finalize the agreement.

Remember that experienced CEO candidates have most likely negotiated a few salary packages during their career. They are usually very knowledgeable and good at negotiations. Don't let ego or emotion get in the way. You will want your next CEO to have confidence when it becomes time to negotiate with the board regarding other strategic issues benefiting your organization.

Alternately, if your final candidate is causing discomfort during negotiations, it may be a signal that this person is not the best fit for your organization. An executive search consultant will provide reasonable and sound advice on all matters related to negotiations.

It is important to take the long-term view. Ask yourself this question, "Will the issues involved in these negotiations matter to us in two or three years?" If the answer is no, then do what you can to find a workable solution that allows both sides to feel like they won. Though salary is usually the biggest issue on the mind of a final candidate, a reasonable incentive package based on performance, additional severance pay, etc., can often bring negotiations to a successful conclusion.

Every step of the negotiation needs to be conducted with integrity so that when you have a signed agreement, both parties are prepared to work together. A few final comments:

- Allow the candidate to win something that is more important to them than to you.

- Offer perhaps a bit more than you originally planned, if necessary. (To offset the extra cost, you could offer more upfront but suggest that their annual salary increase will take place in eighteen months instead of twelve.)

- Make sure everyone comes away feeling like they won.

Be certain the offer with the full terms of employment and compensation package is included in a letter to be signed by the new CEO. The expected starting date should also be included in the letter along with an overview of your expectations of the new CEO. It is also important to include language regarding any agreed-upon severance arrangement and at-will employment status.

Once you receive the signed letter from your new CEO and they have officially notified their current employer, develop a well-written communication plan to announce your new CEO to your stakeholders, both internally and externally. This is a major announcement for your organization and a very exciting time for everyone.

Prior to moving on to our next discussion, I want to address a major issue involving the leadership transition period. Namely, how long should the current CEO remain on the premises when the new CEO begins? Unless there is some special reason or exception, it is my strong recommendation that the new CEO commence their job without the former CEO hanging on.

The idea that the new CEO will need the former CEO to introduce them to staff members and other key stakeholders is ridiculous. Having a current and former CEO in the office together only serves to confuse the transition process. If you feel it is a must to allow the current CEO be part of the transition, limit it to one week or less.

Think of it this way: If you were recently re-married, would you invite your ex-spouse to spend a month with your new spouse to help them acclimate to their new role? I didn't think so.

Now let's turn to our final discussion about how to best onboard your new CEO.

Chapter 9

Onboarding the Candidate

The best and most beautiful things in the world
cannot be seen or even touched,
they must be felt by the heart.

Helen Keller

Everyone in the board room is thrilled to learn that your selected candidate has accepted the offer to become your next chief executive officer. The members of the search committee are ecstatic and relieved to know the new CEO is finally in place. Volunteers are tripping over each other to hand over the keys, get out of the way, and go back to their own jobs.

Not so fast. To ensure that your new chief executive succeeds in their job, the board needs to think differently about this period of transition. According to a recent survey, almost 50% of new CEOs reported getting little or no support from their boards after starting their new job. A better approach is to invest in onboarding your new chief executive officer.

"Onboarding" refers to preparing the CEO to adjust to the social, cultural and professional components of their new role. The greater the investment of your board's time in the executive's onboarding process, the quicker your new CEO will be leading your organization successfully into the future.

I know how exhausting the search process can be, especially for those who served on the search committee. A positive onboarding process will maximize the return on investment, getting the most out of the resources and time you committed to the search and hiring process.

Consider the following as you design the onboarding process:

- How does the board expect the CEO to communicate with them?

- How often does the board chair want to meet or speak with the new CEO? Monthly? Weekly?

- What are the most important items to add to the new CEO's calendar for the first few weeks?

- What are the most pressing strategic issues the board wants the CEO to immediately address?

- What are the key cultural issues facing the organization related to any expected resistance to change?

- Which senior team members have performance improvement issues the new CEO should know about up-front?

- What key external stakeholders (donors, business, civic and community leaders) should the new CEO schedule time to meet with in the first few months?

- What does the CEO need from the board and their senior team to ensure a successful transition?

- What measures or milestones will the board and the new CEO agree to for the first year? The next three to five years?

- How will the CEO be evaluated by the board?

The new CEO needs to take responsibility in the onboarding process as well. Both CEO and board should spend time together, collectively setting the organization's strategic agenda for the future and determining how the board and CEO will share power and decision making.

In my book, *The Nonprofit Board Therapist*, I described the four stages or life cycles of board governance:

- Founding
- Fiduciary
- Strategic
- Leadership

During onboarding, it is important for the CEO and board chair to delve more deeply into an analysis of where your organization is on this continuum. Ideally, you began this discussion during the interview process. A mutual understanding of your organization's life cycle will help you to share also an understanding of how key strategic decisions will be made going forward.

A few years ago, *The Nonprofit Times* included an article from the *Stanford Social Information Review* that highlighted the importance of onboarding for new chief executives in the nonprofit sector. The article's author pointed out that many nonprofit chief executives are in the CEO position for the first time and, after experiencing an enjoyable honeymoon period, they have a significant drop in job satisfaction and contentment in working with their board. In some cases, CEOs even reported experiencing fear and insomnia as they confronted job demands they did not anticipate.

The article went on to state that approximately one-third of all new CEOs follow a leader who was fired or forced out, suggesting that nonprofit boards and executives are frequently out of sync when it comes to performance expectations.

From my personal experience as a leadership coach and executive search consultant, I have found it remarkable how many nonprofit boards do not provide an annual performance evaluation of their chief executives. Linking the new executive's development to your organization's strategic goals and the social impact it wants to achieve will dramatically increase the odds of success for your new CEO.

We began this book discussing how recruiting your next CEO will be the most important responsibility you will ever undertake as a board member. Now that you have gone through the search process and hired your new chief executive leader, you have the added responsibility of investing the appropriate amount of time and energy in onboarding your new CEO.

Onboarding will help to ensure that your organization benefits from your new CEO's expertise, experience and knowledge for many years to come.

Our lives are enriched every day by the positive social impact that America's nonprofit sector creates in our communities. Regardless of your organization's particular mission, it is my hope that this book provided you and your fellow board members with the knowledge, confidence and strategies to select the best CEO to lead your organization forward.

A Note from the Author

Thank you for reading *A Guide to Recruiting Your Next CEO*. If you've enjoyed this book, please leave a review on your favorite review site. It helps me reach more people so they too can recruit the right chief executive officer to lead their organization into the future.

If you haven't already downloaded the *Final Candidate Evaluation Matrix*, you may want to do so now. It will help you objectively evaluate the suitability of candidates as you draw nearer to making your final decision. You can request your copy at denniscmiller.com/candidatescore.

You may also want to download the *Reference Checking Matrix* as well from denniscmiller.com/references to capture your thoughts and impressions while checking a candidate's references.

Once again, I hope you've enjoyed reading this book. I wish you much success in finding the right CEO for your organization. to capture your thoughts and impressions while checking a candidate's references. Once again, I hope you've enjoyed reading this book. I wish you much success in finding the right CEO for your organization.

Hiring and onboarding a CEO is one of the most important (and challenging) actions a board will ever undertake. Choosing a poor match will have a significant impact on your organization's abilities to follow through on its mission.

In Chapter 2, I talked about the importance of being clear what your strategic vision is before hiring your next CEO. This way, you can ensure that the candidate you choose has the skill sets necessary to help you fulfill that vision.

One of my earlier books goes into much more detail regarding the importance of strategic alignment within your organization. If this is an area your board wants to explore before working on its position profile for the next CEO, you'll find an excerpt from *The Power of Strategic Alignment* in the following pages.

An Excerpt from…
The Power of Strategic Alignment

I have been very fortunate to work with many great people and organizations over the past thirty plus years in the nonprofit sector. All of the executive directors, board members, corporate and foundation officers, volunteers, donors and professional colleagues that I have worked with have had a very positive impact on me. I guess you can say that I have been truly blessed to be associated with such great people. What impresses me the most is their passion and commitment to make a difference in the lives of others. They truly care about others and work tremendously long hours to generate a positive social impact in their communities, often with little financial reward. Their commitment to their respective mission and determination to succeed despite the ever-increasing challenges and obstacles inspires me. They are truly some of the most wonderful people I know.

What concerns me the most, however, is how many of them continue to spend an inordinate amount of time and energy without the results and successes they hoped to achieve for their respective organizations. Regardless of their purposeful missions and great causes, many struggle to fully engage their boards and stakeholders and develop the resources to survive, let alone succeed or excel. I believe strongly that there is a new smarter way to achieve success in the nonprofit sector.

In my first book, *A Guide to Achieving New Heights: The Four Pillars of Successful Nonprofit Leadership*, my goal was to provide an inspirational and educational book on how to unlock the leadership potential of chief executives, board members and those who aspire to leadership positions in the nonprofit sector. In my second book, *The Nonprofit Board Therapist: A Guide to Unlocking Your Organization's True Potential*, my goal was to provide a roadmap for how to productively integrate effective board governance, inspiring leadership, powerful visionary thinking and philanthropic success.

In *The Power of Strategic Alignment: A Guide to Energizing Leadership and Maximizing Potential in Today's Nonprofit Organizations*, I will identify the key steps necessary to go beyond the traditional strategic planning process to achieve long-term success and sustainability. This innovative concept is called "strategic alignment," which refers to the process of aligning all stakeholders, both internally and externally, to be focused and committed to achieving one goal: the organization's vision. In addition, the concept requires the development of new competencies and non-traditional skill sets for both executive and board leadership.

The traditional way most nonprofit organizations embark on their strategic planning process often begins with high hopes, but concludes in disappointment with little achieved and the report often ending up sitting on some executive's shelf collecting dust. This disappointment is commonly the result of most strategic plans lacking the following four components:

- An upfront, comprehensive assessment of the organization to identify key strengths and crucial areas of needed improvement;

- A clear vision with established measures of successful progress to align the entire organization's efforts;

- A comprehensive funding plan to secure the necessary resources, and;

- A detailed plan for implementation and execution with buy-in from both the board and staff.

For nearly a decade, I have performed numerous organizational and board performance assessment studies. What became very obvious to me when conducting these assessments was the absolute lack of any real alignment of the organization in pursuit of an agreed-upon vision. Many times the organization did not have a vision or future direction to follow. Even those who indicated they had a vision statement admitted it was often not more than a meaningless statement about "becoming all things to all people" or something like that. There was no organized plan of action to incorporate the work of the board and the efforts of the leadership team and staff toward this vision. Everyone worked very hard on many strategic initiatives but they were not all aligned toward a common goal. Nor was their culture of performance aligned toward the effort of collaboration and respect. To my amazement, far too many leadership teams never even take the time to collectively discuss the many strategic issues facing their own organization. Never. They are all too busy. No wonder they struggle to survive, let alone succeed!

It became apparent to me that to successfully assist an organization in truly developing a strategic plan, all of their goals and actions necessary to achieve a vision have to be fully aligned. The entire organization, including the work of the board, leadership and staff, has to be restructured to require individual goals to be fully aligned with organizational goals. Everyone has to be on the same page and motivated toward the one compelling goal—achieving the organization's vision. In essence, the organization needs to be in strategic alignment. Too many organizations focus solely on the external environmental challenges during the strategic planning when the major reason most organizations fail is their inability to address their internal obstacles. The overwhelming reason most nonprofit organizations fail is the result of not adequately addressing their internal issues and not because of their response to the changing environmental landscape of the sector. Internal obstacles often include the lack of trust and respect among senior managers, stale programs, board members who have stayed far too long, and the lack of contemporary leadership skill sets. An organization needs to honestly address both challenges, internal and external, in order to be in strategic alignment.

The "silo mentality" that so many organizations were working under is no longer acceptable and actually is extremely detrimental to their very survival. Far worse, too many organizations have unresolved internal issues and conflicts preventing them from working more effectively together. The idea of a senior management team not talking, respecting or trusting each other has to be dealt with "head on" and eliminated. The culture of "my needs first" has to be transformed to "those we serve first." There are enough external obstacles that every organization has to face, but to also have to deal constantly with their internal obstacles of personality and egos is wasting valuable energy and time. A new effort to fully align the entire organization has to be developed.

I begin to facilitate my strategic planning clients by first performing an organization-wide assessment to determine their strategic alignment, or lack thereof, with their vision. Everything began to make more sense when I realized they needed a "coach and facilitator" to help with the implementation of their strategic alignment.

Recently, I asked a number of clients who completed their strategic planning process with me under my new "strategic alignment approach" to answer, "What has the process done for you?" The typical responses that I expected were, "It provided us with a clear path forward" or "helped transform the organization" or "really engaged our board." I have heard these responses before and I was always very pleased to hear them express their satisfaction with my work. However, I began to hear from many of my clients that "you helped revitalize our organization." They told me that they now felt a greater sense of confidence to achieve their strategic goals and the know-how to accomplish them. They indicated that my new process of strategic alignment reenergized the entire board and staff and they were excited "to know who they were and where they were going."

I will also describe the new competencies and skill sets required of today's nonprofit leaders as well as the characteristics of high-performing nonprofit boards. Today, more than ever before, the chief executive and board must be true partners in leading the organization forward to generate the positive social impact needed in their communities. In order for your organization to successfully pursue its vision and goals, it must be in strategic alignment.

Organizations that are in strategic alignment have these characteristics:

- Strong organizational self-knowledge
- Engaged key stakeholders

- Inspiring vision
- Entrepreneurial Leaders
- High-performing boards
- Impactful programs and service
- Achievement- and outcome-driven
- Investors seeking to contribute
- Commitment to continuous improvement
- Recognized for excellence

As you read this book, you will learn how to dramatically increase your organizational alignment and begin to achieve new and dramatic levels of success. You will come away from reading this book with:

- A new way to embark on a more effective strategic planning process to build organizational capacity for long-term sustainability.

- The hope, courage and motivation to achieve dramatically better results for your organization.

- A greater sense of purpose and self-confidence to empower you to feel more hopeful and passionate and less stressful about what you need to do.

- Being able to approach your work with a higher level of energy and a positive attitude knowing the best practices of others and how to implement them.

- Knowing how to truly revitalize and "impart new life to your organization" through strategic alignment.

There may be a particular chapter in *The Power of Strategic Alignment* that you may want to read first, but you should read this book in its entirety. In this way, you will gain a much better understanding of how to successfully initiate and complete the strategic planning process. This book includes the following chapters:

- The Assessment – How to Discover Your Organization's Organizational Soul
- The Vision – What Are Your Dreams
- The Process – How to Build Your Plan
- Executive Leadership – Why Today's CEO Means Chief Entrepreneurial Officer
- High-Performing Boards – How to Fully Engage Your Board
- Impactful Programs and Services – When to Collaborate, Affiliate or Merge
- The Positive Brand – What Do People Know Us For
- Seeking Investors, Not Just Funders – Why Giving to Success Makes $ense
- Successfully Executing the Plan – How to Build the Bicycle While Riding It

I hope you enjoy this book and come away revitalized.

. . .

To read the rest of *The Power of Strategic Alignment*, visit emeraldlakebooks.com/dmalignment.

Acknowledgments

I want to begin by thanking my longtime colleague and friend, Michele Hickey, for encouraging me to write this book and for her wonderful job as editor. Michele has a special gift for making suggestions that always improve my writing and grammar. I owe Michele a great deal of gratitude for her tireless efforts to make me look good as a writer.

I especially want to thank my colleagues at The Nonprofit Search Group, especially Phil Beekman, Susie Delaporte and Jay Angeletti. A special thank you to my BFF David Flood as well.

I also want to thank Tara Alemany, my publisher at Emerald Lake Books, and Mark Gerber, Art Director, for their professionalism and encouragement to publish this book.

Finally, I want to thank my wife, Gladys, for always encouraging and supporting me to follow my passion in pursuit of my dreams.

About the Author

Dennis C. Miller is a nationally recognized strategic leadership coach and executive search consultant with more than thirty-five years of experience working with nonprofit board leadership and chief executives across the country. Dennis is also an expert in board governance, leadership development, philanthropy and succession planning. In addition, he is a sought-after motivational speaker, retreat facilitator, and board and leadership performance coach.

Dennis' experience working with hundreds of nonprofit organizations has provided him with the knowledge and insights to understand the competencies required of today's nonprofit leadership, whether as chief executive officer, chief operating officer or chief development officer. As Managing Director of The Nonprofit Search Group, he recruits executives who can inspire their organization to achieve greater levels of success and measurable achievements.

As the former president and chief executive officer of a major medical center and foundation in New Jersey, his reputation as a respected healthcare executive resulted in numerous honors, including the status of Fellow in the American College of Health Executives. He has served as a member of the Board of Trustees for the New Jersey Council of Teaching Hospitals, Chaired the Board of Trustees for the

Center for Health Affairs, Inc. in Princeton, and served in a leadership capacity on many other nonprofit boards.

Dennis obtained his undergraduate degree from Rutgers University and Master's degree in Public Health Administration from Columbia University's Mailman School of Public Health.

Passionate about leadership and governance, Dennis was the Founder of the Center for Excellence in Leadership, Governance and Philanthropy at Fairleigh Dickinson University, the largest private university in New Jersey. He served as the Center's Executive Director from 2012 to 2016. He was also the Chairman of the Board of Trustees for Saint Joseph's Regional High School in Montvale, New Jersey, a highly respected academic college preparatory school. He served as Chairman of their Profiles in Excellence Capital Campaign and was recently inducted into the school's Green Knights Hall of Fame.

Dennis is the author of three books on nonprofit organization success:

- ***A Guide to Achieving New Heights***:
  The Four Pillars of Successful Nonprofit Leadership

- ***The Nonprofit Board Therapist***:
  A Guide to Unlocking Your Organization's True Potential

- ***The Power of Strategic Alignment***:
  A Guide to Energizing Leadership and Maximizing Potential in Today's Nonprofit Organizations.

Dennis is also a regular columnist for many of America's leading nonprofit business publications and blogs.

With his autobiography, *Moppin' Floors to CEO: From Hopelessness and Failure to Happiness and Success,* Dennis mixes together the right ingredients for an engaging, illuminating and compelling memoir, providing a gut-honest recount of his highly eventful life with engaging stories and valuable life lessons. Dennis shows how anyone, including a troubled kid from New Jersey, can overcome seemingly insurmountable obstacles, make it to the top and live a happy and fulfilling life.

Dennis can be contacted at
dennis@denniscmiller.com.

Bibliography

Boogaard, Kat. "9 Must-Ask Interview Questions for Executive Directors & Other Nonprofit Leadership Roles." CauseVox. https://www.causevox.com/blog/nonprofit-interview-questions/ (posted August 1, 2016).

Bradt, George. "Board Best Practices in Onboarding a New CEO." Forbes. https://www.forbes.com/sites/georgebradt/2016/09/06/board-best-practices-in-onboarding-a-new-ceo/ (posted September 6, 2016).

Francis, Sylvia and Katie Donovan. "Should HR Ask for Job Candidates' Salary Histories?" Society for Human Resource Management. https://www.shrm.org/hr-today/news/hr-magazine/0416/pages/should-hr-ask-for-job-candidates-salary-histories.aspx (posted April 1, 2016).

Hesse, Andreas. "How to Conduct an Effective Reference Check." Clear HR Consulting Inc. https://clearhrconsulting.com/blog/hr-smalltalk/conduct-effective-reference-check/ (posted May 10, 2016).

Knight, Rebecca. "The Right Way to Check Someone's References." Harvard Business Review. https://hbr.org/2016/07/the-right-way-to-check-someones-references (posted July 29, 2016).

McKee, Annie. "How to Hire for Emotional Intelligence." Harvard Business Review. https://hbr.org/2016/02/how-to-hire-for-emotional-intelligence (posted February 5, 2016).

Ryan, Liz. "Ten Ways Employers Screen Out the Best Candidates." Forbes. https://www.forbes.com/sites/lizryan/2016/10/18/ten-ways-employers-screen-out-the-best-candidates/ (posted October 18, 2016).

Slezak, Paul. "7 Tips for Conducting a Proper Reference Check." RecruitLoop. http://recruitloop.com/blog/7-ways-to-really-conduct-a-reference-check/ (posted January 27, 2016).

Sun, Carolyn. "7 Interview Questions That Determine Emotional Intelligence." Entrepreneur. https://www.entrepreneur.com/slideshow/299813 (posted March 8. 2016).

Youshaei, Jon. "6 Great Secrets of Great Resumes, Backed by Psychology." Forbes. https://www.forbes.com/sites/jonyoushaei/2014/08/27/resumes (posted August 27, 2014).

Zielinski, Dave. "Effective Assessments. Society for Human Resource Management." https://www.shrm.org/hr-today/news/hr-magazine/pages/0111zielinski.aspx (posted January 1, 2011).

Index

O

O'Leary, George, 55–56
onboarding, 63–66

P

plans
  business, 13
  fundraising, 11
  implementation, 3
  resource, 11
problem solving, 45
professional associations, 32

R

recommendations. *See* candidates, recommended
reference checks, 4, 26, 28–29, 48–53, 56
relationship
  CEO and board, 12–13
  search committee and firm, 29
relationship builder, 19, 21
relocations, 32
resumes
  gap in work history, 36–37
  screening, 34–35

S

salary, 24, 26, 33, 39, 57–60
  history, 38
sample questions, 1, 9, 24, 38, 45, 53
screening process, 26, 31, 34, 38
search

V

W

For more great books, visit us at
emeraldlakebooks.com

Printed in Great Britain
by Amazon